ISAAC ASIMOV'S
Pioneers of Science and Exploration

HENRY HUDSON

Arctic Explorer and North American Adventurer

by Isaac Asimov
and Elizabeth Kaplan

Gareth Stevens Children's Books
MILWAUKEE

For a free color catalog describing Gareth Stevens' list of high-quality children's books, call 1-800-341-3569 (USA) or 1-800-461-9120 (Canada).

Picture Credits

From the American Geographical Society Collection, Golda Meir Library, University of Wisconsin-Milwaukee 23; The Bridgeman Art Library 8-9; © 1991 Gareth Stevens, Inc. 10; Mary Evans Picture Library 11, 18 (upper), 28, 30, 33, 44; New York State Department of Economic Development 31; The Ontario Government Ministry of Tourism and Recreation 38-39.
The publishers especially wish to thank the employees of the Spice House of Milwaukee, Wisconsin, for their assistance.

Library of Congress Cataloging-in-Publication Data

Asimov, Isaac, 1920-
    Henry Hudson : Arctic explorer and North American adventurer / by Isaac Asimov and Elizabeth Kaplan.
       p. cm. — (Isaac Asimov's pioneers of exploration)
    Includes bibliographical references and index.
    Summary: Describes the adventures of the seventeenth-century English explorer, from his search for a short route from Europe to the Orient to his mysterious disappearance after members of his crew mutinied.
    ISBN 0-8368-0558-5
    1. Hudson, Henry, d. 1611—Juvenile literature. 2. Explorers—America—Biography—Juvenile literature. 3. Explorers—England—Biography—Juvenile literature. 4. America—Discovery and exploration—English—Juvenile literature. 5. Hudson Bay—Discovery and exploration—English—Juvenile literature. [1. Hudson, Henry, d. 1611. 2. Explorers.] I. Kaplan, Elizabeth, 1956- . II. Title. III. Series: Asimov, Isaac, 1920- Isaac Asimov's pioneers of exploration.
E129.H8A84   1991
910'.92—dc20   [B]   [92]   90-23948

A Gareth Stevens Children's Books edition

Edited, designed, and produced by
Gareth Stevens Children's Books
1555 North RiverCenter Drive, Suite 201
Milwaukee, Wisconsin 53212, USA

Series editors: Amy Bauman and Elizabeth Kaplan
Editorial assistant: Scott Enk
Series designer: Kristi Ludwig
Picture researcher: Daniel Helminak
Picture research assistant: Diane Laska
Illustrator: K. Dyble Thompson
Map designer: Mark Mille

Printed in the United States of America

1 2 3 4 5 6 7 8 9 95 94 93 92 91

CONTENTS

THE MYSTERIOUS HENRY HUDSON

Rising above the majestic Hudson River in the state of New York is a range of mountains called the Catskills. According to legend, a band of strange, ragged men used to roam these mountains playing ninepins, an early bowling game. It was said that what people thought was thunder rumbling through the hills was really the noise of the men's wild bowling matches. Storytellers also claim that the leader of these men was the ghost of the English explorer Henry Hudson.

In the early 1600s, Henry Hudson sailed the arctic waters above Europe and North America. He battled icebergs off the northern coast of Russia. He explored the Hudson River and wrote glowing descriptions of the lands along its banks. He crossed huge Hudson Bay in present-day Canada and spent the winter locked to its icy shore. Even today, we have detailed records of these exciting expeditions.

Such records of Henry Hudson's early life, however, do not exist. We don't know when Hudson was born. We don't know what kind of family he grew up in. We don't know what he looked like or where he went to school. Until we see him on the deck of a ship, in 1607, headed for the unknown seas north of Europe, his life has been almost a complete mystery. But today's historians are able to piece together clues about people like Henry Hudson. Because of their work, the story of Hudson's life is no longer a mystery.

1

AN APPETITE FOR EXPLORING

Henry Hudson was probably born in London, England, sometime in the early 1570s. He may have been the son of a sea captain or a merchant. He probably was the grandson of one of the aldermen of London, also named Henry Hudson. The elder Henry Hudson helped start the Muscovy Company.

This English business venture had two goals. One goal was to trade English wool for Russian furs, gold, and other valuable items. The other goal was to find a short route to the trading ports of China.

Perhaps it was his grandfather who awakened young Henry Hudson's appetite for exploring. From his grandfather, he might have heard about the adventures of brave sea captains who had sailed the northern seas. He might have heard tales from the sailors themselves as they docked on the wharves of the Thames River. Some historians even think that as a teenager, Henry Hudson might have sailed to the shores of North America with English explorer John Davis.

In 1587, Davis led an expedition to find a waterway across North America that would connect the Atlantic and Pacific oceans. Although no one knew for sure, many people thought that such a northwest passage existed. Late in the summer, Davis and his crew sailed into a channel filled with whirlpools and swirling ice. Davis didn't have time to sail all the way through the channel before winter closed in. But he described the channel, which he called Furious Overfall, as a possible northwest passage.

A map from the late 1500s shows what was thought to be the world's geography. Among other features, the map shows Terra Australis, the "land of the south." Scientists of the day were sure this mass had to exist to balance the masses of land above the equator.

If young Henry Hudson sailed on this voyage, he might have dreamed of someday crossing this dangerous channel. If Hudson didn't go with Davis, he might have read Davis's account of his harrowing voyage. Whatever the influence, Hudson was an expert navigator by the time he was in his early thirties. In 1607, the leaders of the Muscovy Company hired him to find a new trade route to the Orient — the faraway lands of India and China.

2

OVER THE POLE

Walking through London in the early 1600s wasn't always a pleasant experience. The streets were filled with garbage that people simply threw out of their windows. The garbage rotted where it fell, creating a horrible odor.

The smells floating out of London's kitchens wouldn't have been much sweeter. In the seventeenth century, people had no way to properly preserve food. Things spoiled quickly. Sometimes, the only way to make meals taste better was to cover up the flavor of spoiled food with a sprinkling of spices such as cinnamon, pepper, cloves, and nutmeg.

But these prized spices were expensive. They had to be imported all the way from India and China. In the early 1600s, the Arabs and Italians controlled the land route to the Orient. The Portuguese controlled the sea route around Africa. The English paid dearly for spices that the Italians and the Portuguese sold them. Before long, the English decided that they wanted a share of the spice trade. They needed to find a new sea route to the Orient.

By Hudson's time, spices were used throughout Europe. Many were used for flavoring, but some could also be used to help preserve food.

In the 1600s, London was a booming city and a center of business and culture. Its streets were exciting, but they were also crowded, dirty, and sometimes dangerous.

Enter Henry Hudson. Hudson had a theory. He figured that the shortest route to the Orient from England would be one that traveled directly over the North Pole. Of course, Hudson knew nothing about the frozen mantle of snow and ice that covers the polar region. He supposed that the summer sun, which doesn't set at the North Pole, would make the climate as agreeable as that of Europe. Hudson's argument convinced the leaders of the Muscovy Company. They agreed to back his voyage and gave him a ship called the *Hopewell*. On May 1, 1607, Henry Hudson set sail for the North Pole.

Right: Henry Hudson's routes covered much of the globe. By the time of his death, he had explored a broad territory from the southeastern coastal waters of the present-day United States all the way north to the Arctic Ocean.
Inset: This diagram gives an idea of the route Hudson thought he could sail to the Orient. Without accurate maps, he had no way of knowing that ice would stop him from traveling directly over the North Pole.

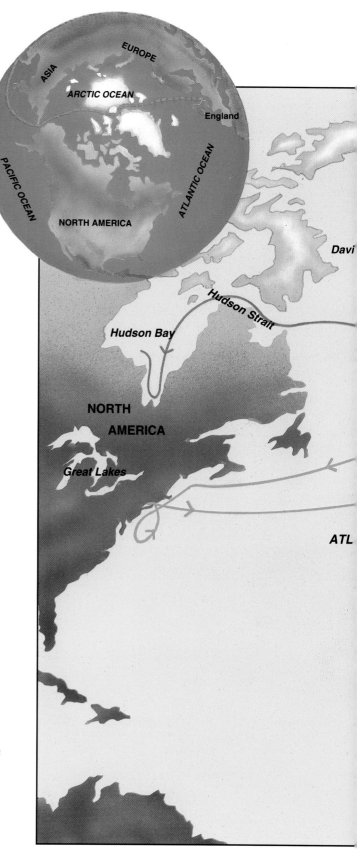

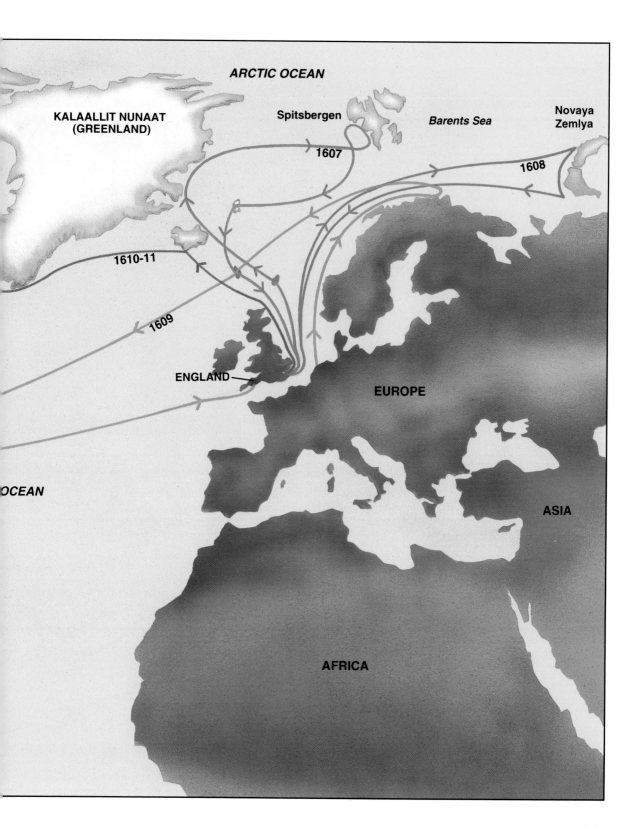

ARCTIC OCEAN

KALAALLIT NUNAAT
(GREENLAND)

Spitsbergen

Barents Sea

Novaya
Zemlya

1607

1608

1610-11

1609

ENGLAND

EUROPE

ASIA

OCEAN

AFRICA

On board the *Hopewell*, Hudson and his crew led a life of hardship. Their main food was a dense biscuit called hardtack. Stews of pickled meat, carrots, onions, and barley were the daily fare. Water, stored in casks, soon became green with algae.

Sailing the *Hopewell* in the cold northern oceans was grueling work. The sails were hard to handle and stiffened with frost. The men's hands

Life aboard a sailing ship was hard. Crew members had little space for themselves and most slept in hammocks strung wherever there was room.

became chapped and frozen from hauling in the icy ropes. The *Hopewell*, made for sailing in calmer waters, rocked crazily with the arctic swells.

After a hard day on the rigging, the sailors bedded down in flimsy hammocks. As the ship rolled, the hanging beds swayed back and forth like a clock's pendulum. Even the captain's quarters were spare. Hudson slept in a small, shelflike bed suspended from the wall. In such rough, cramped conditions, Hudson and his crew spent months, buffeted by the icy, gray waves.

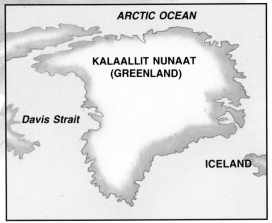

Hudson's first voyage took him north as far as Kalaallit Nunaat (Greenland) and the Arctic Ocean.

On leaving England, the *Hopewell* headed northwest, slipping by the Faeroe Islands and Iceland. After sailing for six weeks, Hudson and crew sighted the coast of Kalaallit Nunaat (formerly Greenland). The weather was terrible. Rain froze on the decks, and fog closed in around the ship. Nevertheless, the *Hopewell* continued northward. A week later, the fog lifted. Hudson spotted the mountains of Kalaallit Nunaat looming to the west, but his maps showed only water. The sailors spent the next two weeks mapping the coast of this monstrous, frozen island.

Packs of ice eventually forced Hudson to change course. He turned northeast and soon reached a group of islands that Dutch explorers had named Spitsbergen. For several weeks, the *Hopewell* cruised through the islands where the sailors saw seals and walrus sunning themselves on

rocks. The men were amazed by the tiny trees that dotted the windswept land. But the biggest surprise came when they sailed into a sheltered bay where the whales were so thick that they rubbed against the ship. Hudson named the cove Whales Bay.

Exploring the land, the sailors found deer antlers, flocks of plump geese, and a spring of clear water. This abundant game and the warm weather in Whales Bay made Hudson think that his theory about the North Pole would prove true. But within a few days the *Hopewell* was packed in by ice. Hudson steered his ship south, but ten days later, its path was blocked by another groaning wall of ice. Hudson realized that there was no way through to the North Pole. Early in August, he turned back for England. The *Hopewell* sailed into London in mid-September. Although his first attempt to find a passage to the Orient had failed, Hudson was not defeated.

3

THE NORTHEAST PASSAGE

Although Hudson did not think his first voyage a success, his reports of whales off of Spitsbergen had opened England to whaling. The products possible through whaling made this discovery almost as valuable as the spices a new route to the Orient would have brought the country. Some products that come from whales are shown here.

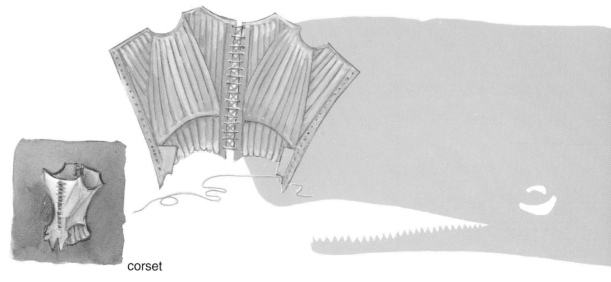

corset

Hudson's reports of the uncountable numbers of whales off the Spitsbergen islands pleased his backers at the Muscovy Company. Whale blubber and whalebone were valued throughout Europe. The blubber was used for making soap, fuel for oil lamps, and grease for carriage wheels. Whalebone was cut to make corsets — women's undergarments that molded the body to an hourglass shape.

Within a few months of Hudson's return, the Muscovy Company was enlisting sailors to go to Spitsbergen to launch England's whaling industry. The company asked Hudson to lead the venture. But Hudson wanted to continue searching for a route to the Orient. The Muscovy Company backed him again. This time Hudson planned to look for a passage running northeast to China and India. Such a passage, along the northern coast of Russia, would allow England to trade with both Russia and the Orient.

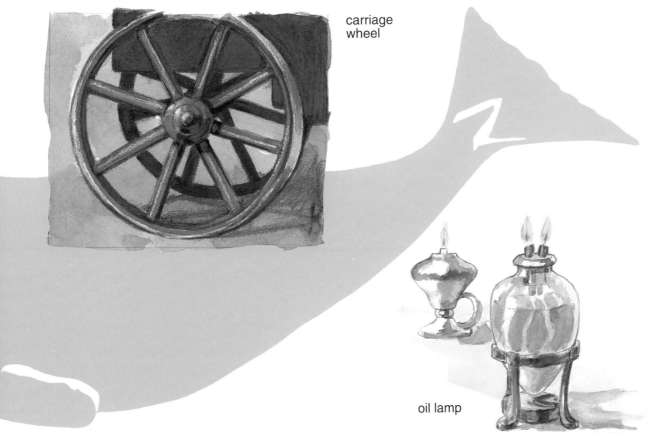

carriage wheel

oil lamp

CLOSE-UP ON A SAILING SHIP

The ship pictured here is a galleon, similar to the kind of ship that Henry Hudson sailed. This ship, which was developed in the sixteenth century, averaged about 135 feet (41 m) long. This would be about twice as long as a modern semitrailer, which stretches to a length of about 65 feet (20 m).

KEY

1. Stern
2. Rudder
3. Bonadventure mizzenmast
4. Mizzenmast
5. Mainmast
6. Shrouds
7. Cannons
8. Bilge
9. Foremast
10. Anchor
11. Bow or stern
12. Bowsprit
13. Figurehead

9

6

12

13

7

10

11

8

On his second voyage, Hudson sailed to the islands of Novaya Zemlya.

Hudson prepared to sail in April of 1608. To strengthen the *Hopewell* for the rigorous voyage, he had the ship's hull reinforced with extra planks of wood. He also replaced the old mast with a stronger, thicker one. Finally, he purchased a sturdy rowboat for exploring ice-encrusted shores.

Even more important than these preparations was choosing the crew. Few of the sailors who had gone on Hudson's first voyage were available for the second. In Hudson's crew of fourteen, only three sailors had sailed with him to the Arctic before.

For his new first mate, Hudson chose a tough, experienced sailor named Robert Juet. On a ship, the first mate took command whenever the captain was resting or asleep. For this reason, it was important that the captain pick a first mate that he could trust. Unfortunately, Juet turned out to be a sneaky man who seemed to dislike Hudson.

Nevertheless, the second voyage began without trouble. The *Hopewell* left London on April 22, 1608. After sailing northeast for a month, Hudson and his crew rounded the northern coast of Norway at the end of May. The *Hopewell* continued through the Barents Sea, avoiding icebergs that rose on the horizon.

By the end of June, the *Hopewell* reached the islands called Novaya Zemlya. Hudson sailed up the west coast of one of the islands, hoping to find a channel through it. However, an ice barrier forced him to turn around and sail southward. He continued searching for a passageway through the landmass until the beginning of July. Along the way, the crew explored the coast of Novaya Zemlya, enjoying the

Hudson and his crew spent days exploring the pair of islands known as Novaya Zemlya. These islands are located off the northern coast of the Soviet Union. Today, these remote islands are the site of Soviet nuclear testing.

warm sunshine, the sweet-smelling alpine flowers, and the plentiful geese and ducks they shot for food.

In early July, the weather turned cold and stormy. Hudson still had not found a channel across Novaya Zemlya. Sadly, he turned the *Hopewell* around and headed the ship westward.

But if the crew thought they were returning home, Hudson had other ideas. He wanted to sail to North America and search for the Furious Overfall. But he kept his plan a secret.

By the end of July, the crew realized that they were headed west across the Atlantic. The first mate, Juet, confronted the captain on his plans. Hudson confessed that he wanted to sail to North America and explore. The crew threatened to mutiny unless Hudson turned the ship around and headed home. They then forced Hudson to sign a paper saying that he was returning home of his own free will.

As captain, Hudson had the right to punish anyone who refused to obey him. He could even put disobedient sailors to death. In giving in to his crew, Hudson probably lost their respect. When the *Hopewell* reached London in late August, however, neither Hudson nor the crew mentioned the troubles at sea.

That fall, Hudson delivered his report to the Muscovy Company. Like Hudson, the leaders of the Muscovy Company were disappointed in the outcome of the voyage. They dismissed Henry Hudson from their service.

In his cabin, Hudson gloomily ponders the outcome of his second voyage.

4

SURPRISE VISIT TO NORTH AMERICA

Losing his job depressed Hudson. Exploring was his passion. Finding a passage to the Orient had become his life's goal. Luckily, Hudson soon had a new offer. Emanuel van Meteran, a Dutch citizen living in London, came to him with an idea. The Dutch East Indies Company, a trading company in Holland, wanted to find a short route to India and China. Perhaps Hudson could get the Dutch to hire him for another voyage. Hudson liked the idea. Within a few months, he was on his way to Amsterdam to talk with the trading company.

When Hudson reached Amsterdam, the Dutch delayed meeting with him. They made no promises about giving him a job. Hudson decided to talk to the French, who were also eager to expand their trade routes. When the Dutch heard of Hudson's plans, they suddenly got serious about hiring him. In January 1609, Hudson signed a contract with the Dutch. According to the agreement, Hudson was to explore the area around Novaya Zemlya, the island he had explored on his second voyage, for a passage to the Orient.

For his crew, Hudson hired some men who had sailed with him before. For example, Robert Juet signed on again. However, Hudson's contract said that half the crew had to be from Holland. This was a problem. Hudson didn't speak Dutch. So he relied on a friend who had never been to sea to do the hiring for him.

Another problem Hudson faced was the ship that the Dutch provided. This ship, the *Half Moon*, was smaller and lighter than the *Hopewell*.

It was made for sailing on the sheltered waters around Amsterdam, not on the open seas. Hudson complained about the ship to his Dutch sponsors, but they would not listen. Finally, Hudson settled for the less-than-perfect vessel.

Despite his uncertainties about his ship and crew, Hudson was eager to be exploring again. On April 6, 1609, the *Half Moon* set sail from Amsterdam.

The first part of Hudson's third voyage was full of

difficulties. The weather was cold and stormy. Worse yet, the English and Dutch crew members didn't get along well. They fought over whether meals should include pickled beef, favored by the English, or pickled fish, favored by the Dutch. They quarreled over who should tend the sails when the seas got rough. The Dutch sailors, who were used to sailing in the warm seas of the tropics, went below deck whenever the icy winds began to blow.

Between the squabbles and the squalls, the *Half Moon* progressed slowly. Not until May did the ship round Norway's northern coast. Still, the bad weather and the fighting continued.

In mid-May, Hudson proposed they abandon the voyage in the icy waters above Europe. He wanted to head west to explore the coast of North America. Thankful to leave the cruel cold, the crew united behind the captain, and the *Half Moon* changed course.

The *Half Moon,* with Henry Hudson aboard, sets sail from Amsterdam.

Some of the Indians that Hudson's crew met in North America were friendly, but the Europeans' abuse of the Indians destroyed friendly terms between the two groups.

In less than a month, Hudson crossed the Atlantic, reaching the North American coast of what is now Canada. From there, the *Half Moon* headed south. On the way, the crew fished along the coast's rich banks and traded for furs with the Indians they met. The voyage seemed to be going well.

As they continued southward, however, Hudson's crew began to grow greedy.

This time, however, they did not fight with each other. Instead, they went after the Indians. One night, a group of sailors stole an Indian canoe and paddled to the nearby Indian camp. Flashing their swords and firing their pistols, they charged the camp. The Indians fled into the forest. The sailors stole furs and other valuable items that the Indians had collected to trade. Hudson did nothing to punish

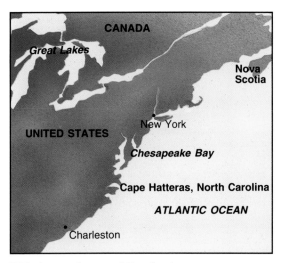

While exploring North America, Hudson sailed the *Half Moon* as far south as modern-day Cape Hatteras, North Carolina.

the sailors for what they had done to the Indians. Instead, the next morning, the *Half Moon* silently slipped away.

Hudson continued sailing along the North American coast for more than a month. On August 19, he turned the *Half Moon* around near a jut of land now known as Cape Hatteras, North Carolina, and headed northward. This time Hudson began searching for a waterway that might connect the Atlantic and Pacific oceans. He sailed up Chesapeake Bay but soon realized that this waterway was

a dead end. He decided the same was true of Delaware Bay.

On September 2, the ship sailed into a magnificent harbor. This, the men were sure, would lead to the Orient. A few days later, they sailed into the entryway of the river known today as the Hudson.

Hudson's first days on the river that bears his name were tragic. On September 6, he sent a crew ahead in a small boat to explore the river's channel. As the men were sailing back to the ship, a canoe full of Indians attacked without warning. A shower of arrows fell all around the Europeans. One man fell dead, pierced in the throat. The next day, the crew buried the sailor and continued up the river more wary than before.

Two days later, Indian canoes again approached the *Half Moon.* When the sailors saw bows and arrows in the canoes, they took no chances. They captured two Indians and sailed on. With Indian hostages aboard, the sailors were confident that no other Indians would attack. No

The Hudson River now (above) and then (opposite).

longer afraid, they treated the hostages badly. Eventually, however, the Indians escaped and swam to shore.

By that time, the *Half Moon* had traveled a long way up the Hudson River. The ship and its crew had passed through what is now New York Harbor. The tall buildings and the giant ocean vessels that line the harbor today would dwarf a ship the size of the little *Half Moon*.

The ship sailed even farther upriver past high cliffs that rose along the river's western shores. Here, the men noted the strange plant and animal life of this rich land that Hudson called "the finest for cultivation that I ever in my life set foot upon." Here, too, relations between the Europeans and the Indians were friendlier. Some of the Indians even invited Hudson and his crew to feasts in their villages. There, Hudson could not help but admire the natives' skills as hunters, builders, fishers, and farmers.

The stunning scenery continued as Hudson sailed into the rugged region where the Catskill Mountains border the river. But the river had narrowed. Hudson began to suspect that this was not a passage to the Orient and sent a small boat ahead to explore.

The sailors confirmed his suspicions. Hudson sadly turned the *Half Moon* around and sailed back downstream. By the beginning of October, the ship reached the mouth of the river. There, the sailors skirmished with a large group of Indians. Among them were probably the two men the sailors had held as hostages. Several Indians were killed in the fighting. Hudson, taking no chances of further battles, sailed on through the night.

When the ship reached the Atlantic, Hudson and his crew held a meeting. Hudson wanted to spend the winter in North America and sail north in the spring to search for the Furious Overfall. Most of the crew wanted to return to Europe for provisions. In the end, they agreed to winter in the British Isles, stock up for another voyage, and return to North America with Hudson the following year.

The *Half Moon* reached the English port of Dartmouth on November 7. Hudson sent word of his explorations to the Dutch at once and began preparing for another voyage. The sailors, however, were at loose ends. Although sworn to secrecy, they began telling stories of their adventures along the mighty river.

Word got back to London. Soon, even King James I had heard of Hudson's discoveries. The king was furious that the work of one of his subjects would benefit another country. He had Henry Hudson arrested and brought back to London. There, Hudson sat in his house, surrounded by soldiers. He waited grimly for the king to bring him to trial on charges of treason.

Opposite: King James I of England was furious to learn that Hudson was sailing for another country.

5

THE ICY BAY

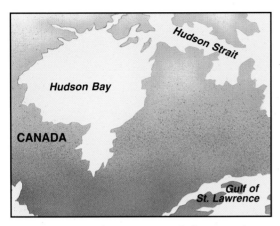

Hudson's final voyage took him to the northern reaches of America. During this trip, Hudson came upon the strait and bay that now bear his name.

When the English people heard about Hudson's arrest, many were outraged. Sailing for another country was not against English law. Most people thought the king was treating Hudson unfairly.

A group of men went to the king and asked him to release the explorer. They convinced King James to allow Hudson to sail under the English flag. The men even raised the money for a ship and crew.

By early spring, Hudson was eagerly preparing for his fourth expedition. For his crew, Hudson hired many men, including Juet, who had sailed with him before. He also hired some men who had never been to sea.

Among them was a rowdy man named Henry Greene. Greene came from a respectable family, but he had fallen in with a rough crowd. He went on drunken sprees, got into fights, and, in general, caused trouble. However, the young man had visited Hudson when he was under arrest and expressed his admiration and sympathy for the captain. Possibly to show his gratitude, Hudson hired Greene.

With all preparations made, Hudson and crew left London

on April 17, 1610, aboard the ship *Discovery*. Sailing went smoothly for the first few weeks, and the *Discovery* made rapid progress crossing the Atlantic. But trouble soon brewed with the crew. Greene got into a fight with another sailor. Juet began spreading rumors about Hudson, saying he had brought Greene aboard to spy on the men. Hudson punished neither Greene nor Juet for their disruptive behavior. Instead, he pushed on for North America.

Supplies are loaded aboard the *Discovery* as Henry Hudson prepares for another voyage.

By June 15 they sighted the large islands off the northern coast of what is today the Canadian province of Quebec. On June 25, they entered the Furious Overfall. This channel, now called Hudson Strait, connects the Atlantic Ocean with the large body of water that has come to be known as Hudson Bay. Its surging tides, treacherous ice

floes, and thick fogs make it challenging even for today's most experienced and well-equipped navigators. Little wonder that the sailors aboard the *Discovery* were terrified by the violent waters. As they sailed the 400 miles (640 km) down this dangerous channel, they pleaded with Hudson to turn back.

Hudson refused to give in to the men's fears. On August 2, the *Discovery* entered a spacious sea of open water. Hudson was sure that he had found a northern route to the Pacific and was on his way to the Orient. For a month, the crew sailed south, hopeful that they would soon be in tropical waters. But then suddenly land cut off their passage. Hudson sailed all along the coast, searching every inlet for a way through.

As fall came on, the crew began to worry. When the sailors came to Juet, he mumbled that the ship was lost and that Hudson would lead them to their deaths. Hudson heard about the trouble and put Juet on trial. A number of men spoke up, saying that the first mate had been whispering against the

captain from the beginning of the voyage. Hudson demoted Juet and punished other members of the crew he felt had been disloyal. He promoted other sailors to take their places. With ice forming on the waters, Hudson, by his actions, had split the crew into two groups. One group supported him. The other held grudges against him.

Inlets off of Hudson Bay often led to rivers that snaked their way into the North American interior. Hudson followed many such leads, only to be disappointed.

Determined to find a northwest passage to the Orient, Henry Hudson searched countless inlets, such as the one seen here, along the North American coast.

The situation on board the ship was menacing, but the approaching winter was even more threatening. By November, the *Discovery* was iced in at the southern tip of Hudson Bay. It was a rocky, barren place. The men had no luck fishing. When they went hunting, they spotted no wild game. They couldn't even find berries to eat. With their stores of food dwindling, the crew faced the future in fear.

The harsh northern winter took its toll on the crew. Many of the men became so sick from the cold and lack of food that they could hardly move. Tempers flared, and more men sided against Hudson. Even Greene, who had avoided conflict with Hudson until then, quarreled with the captain.

The bitterness lasted even after spring began to thaw the frozen bay and warm the land. It wasn't until early June that the *Discovery* came free from the ice. Inspired by the balmy breezes, Hudson headed the ship westward to explore the uncharted waters that he hoped would lead to the Orient. By this time, however, many of the sailors had lost respect for the captain. They wanted only to go home. Greene, Juet, and a few of Hudson's other enemies quietly plotted mutiny.

Hudson and crew spent a winter on Hudson Bay when the *Discovery* became trapped in the ice there. The bitter conditions led the men to plot a mutiny.

On the morning of June 24, three men jumped Hudson as he left his quarters. They bound him hand and foot and lowered him into a small boat. Meantime, the mutineers rounded up the crew members who were still loyal to the captain and those who were ill and forced them to join Hudson. Then they set the small boat adrift, leaving them without food, fresh water, or any other necessities. The brave explorer and his unfortunate band of loyal sailors were never seen or heard from again.

THE LEGACY OF HENRY HUDSON

The remaining crew of the *Discovery* headed back to England. But without Henry Hudson's skill as a navigator, the crew faced a difficult journey. They had to contend with rough seas, attacks by Indians, and the threat of starvation. When the *Discovery* reached England in the autumn of 1611, all the leaders of the mutiny had died. The surviving crew members were never punished for their crimes at sea.

The fate of Henry Hudson himself has remained a mystery. Most historians think the explorer either starved to death on the shores of Hudson Bay or that he drowned in the bay's cold waters. Others claim he and his men made it to shore and eventually intermarried with the Cree Indians in the area. Some people even believe that Hudson's ghost still roams the regions of North America that Hudson explored. Whatever happened to the explorer, his adventures are legendary. He is remembered by people all over the world for exploring the waterways that bear his name: the Hudson River, Hudson Strait, and Hudson Bay. His voyages did much to further European exploration and settlement of North America.

CHRONOLOGY

1570s Henry Hudson is born.

1587 John Davis leads an expedition to North America, searching for a northwest passage between the Atlantic and Pacific oceans. Some historians think that Henry Hudson might have been a member of this crew.

1607 Henry Hudson is hired by the Muscovy Company.
May — Commanding the *Hopewell*, Hudson sets sail, hoping to find a sea route over the North Pole as a shortcut to the Orient.
August — Hudson, blocked by ice at the North Pole, decides to turn back toward England.
September — Hudson and the crew of the *Hopewell* sail into London, England.

1608 **April** — Hudson sets sail on his second voyage for the Muscovy Company. This time, he explores the region north of Russia, looking for a northeast passage to the Orient.
July — Hudson abandons his search for a northeast passage. He heads for North America, secretly planning to explore its coast. When the crew threatens mutiny, Hudson heads back to England.

1609 **January** — Hudson signs on with the Dutch East India Company.
April — Aboard the *Half Moon*, Hudson sets sail on a third voyage to find a new route to the Orient.

May — After the ship is blocked by bad weather in the icy waters along Europe's northern coast, Hudson once again sets sail for the Atlantic coast of North America. During this voyage, Hudson sails up the river now called the Hudson.

1610 The king of England learns of Hudson's explorations for the Dutch and has him arrested. At the request of wealthy merchants, the king pardons Hudson. The merchants then provide Hudson with a ship, the *Discovery*, and provisions for another voyage.
April — Hudson sets sail on his fourth voyage. On this trip, he sails through a channel that is since known as Hudson Strait and explores the body of water known today as Hudson Bay.

1611 Hudson and his crew spend the winter iced in at the southern end of Hudson Bay.
June — The *Discovery* is freed from the ice, and Hudson tries to continue exploring. The crew mutinies and sets Hudson and his loyal crew members adrift in a small boat. Henry Hudson is never seen again.
Fall — The *Discovery* lands in England with the remaining crew. The leaders of the mutiny have all died on the journey. The survivors are never punished for the mutiny.

GLOSSARY

Arctic: The northern reaches of the earth surrounding the North Pole.

blubber: The fat of whales or other sea mammals. Blubber can be eaten or melted into an oil, which once was a widely used source of fuel.

channel: A waterway connecting two great bodies of water. Also, the part of a waterway that is deep enough to allow ships to pass.

Dutch East India Company: A trading company started in 1602 and based in Holland. Its main purpose was to establish and protect Dutch trade in the Orient.

first mate: The second highest ranking officer on a ship.

floe: A large mass of ice floating freely in the sea.

Furious Overfall: A swirling channel of icy water at the mouth of what is now known as the Hudson Strait. The explorer John Davis discovered and named this waterway.

hostage: A person held prisoner by one group in some type of conflict. A hostage is used to make sure that demands are met by the other group.

Muscovy Company: An English trading company of the late 1500s. One of the company's goals was to promote trade with Russia. The company's name, *Muscovy*, is a name for Moscow.

mutiny: A rebellion in which soldiers, sailors, or other subordinates refuse to obey their leader's orders and attempt to overthrow the leader.

ninepins: A form of bowling in which nine pins are used instead of ten. This game is still played in parts of Europe and was brought to America by the Dutch.

Northeast Passage: A sea route connecting the Atlantic and Pacific oceans by way of the northern coasts of Europe and Asia. Early explorers spent years searching for this passage as an alternative route from Europe to the Orient. The passage was discovered in the mid-1600s but was not completely traveled until the 1870s. The passage was impassable for many early ships, such as those of Hudson's time, because of ice.

Northwest Passage: A sea route connecting the Atlantic and Pacific oceans by way of the northern coasts of North America. Early explorers also spent time searching for this passage as another alternate route from Europe to the Orient. Like the Northeast Passage, the use of this waterway was difficult because ice made it impassable for many of the early explorers' ships.

Orient: Literally "the East." This region includes China, Japan, India, and Indonesia, which includes islands that used to be known as the Spice Islands.

seal: A sea mammal of colder regions. This animal has flippers for front limbs and a tail, all of which are used for swimming. The seal has been hunted for centuries for its valuable fur.

treason: A serious crime committed against one's own country.

walrus: A large sea mammal, related to seals, that lives mainly in arctic waters. Like the seal, the walrus is built for swimming and has flippered front limbs and a tail.

THINGS TO READ

The following reading materials will tell you more about Henry Hudson and some of the places that he explored. Some of the titles will also tell you about the times during which Henry Hudson lived. Others will tell you about other great explorers, as well as Henry Hudson.

"The Changing Images of the Northwest Passage." *National Geographic*, August 1990

Elizabethan England. A. H. Dodd (G. P. Putnam's Sons)

Great Adventures That Changed Our World. (Reader's Digest Association)

The Great Explorers. Piers Pennington (Facts on File)

Henry Hudson. Ruth Harley (Troll Associates)

The Hudson: River of History. May McNeer (Garrard)

"Rip Van Winkle" and **"The Legend of Sleepy Hollow."** Washington Irving (Smith Publishers)

PLACES TO WRITE

The following places can tell you more about Henry Hudson and his legacy. When you write, always be specific in your questions. Be sure to include your full name, age, return address, and a return envelope for a reply.

The Hakluyt Society
c/o Map Library, British Library
Great Russell Street
London WC1B 3D6
England

Heritage Canada
P.O. Box 1358, Station B
Ottawa, Ontario K1P 5R4

Hudson's Bay Company
The Secretary
401 Bay Street
Toronto, Ontario M5H 2Y4

National Library of Canada
395 Wellington Street
Ottawa, Ontario K1H 0N4

INDEX

921
HUD   Asimov, Isaac

        Henry Hudson

DATE DUE